NIRVANA

FOR UKULELE

T0079179

Cover photo © Dalle/Atlasicons.com

ISBN 978-1-4950-1096-5

HAL•LEONARD®
CORPORATION

7777 W. BLUEMOUND RD. P.O. BOX 13819 MILWAUKEE, WI 53213

For all works contained herein:
Unauthorized copying, arranging, adapting, recording, Internet posting, public performance,
or other distribution of the printed music in this publication is an infringement of copyright.
Infringers are liable under the law.

Visit Hal Leonard Online at
www.halleonard.com

About a Girl

Words and Music by Kurt Cobain

Copyright © 1989 The End Of Music and Primary Wave Tunes
All Rights Administered by BMG Rights Management (US) LLC
All Rights Reserved   Used by Permission

All Apologies

Words and Music by Kurt Cobain

First note

(Instrumental)

1. What else should I be? _____ All a - pol - o - gies. _
2. *See additional lyrics*

_____ What else could I say? _____

Ev - 'ry - one ___ was gay. ___ What else could I write? _

Copyright © 1993 BMG Platinum Songs, Primary Wave Tunes and The End Of Music
All Rights Administered by BMG Rights Management (US) LLC
All Rights Reserved   Used by Permission

I don't have ___ the right. ___

What else should I be? _____ All a - pol - o - gies. ___

Chorus

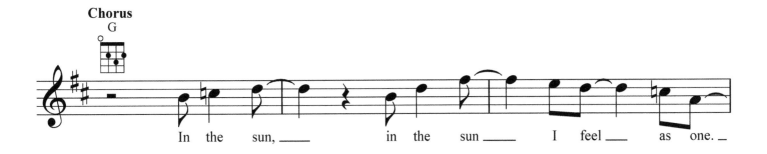

In the sun, ___ in the sun ___ I feel ___ as one. _

___ In the sun, ___ in the sun ___ I'm

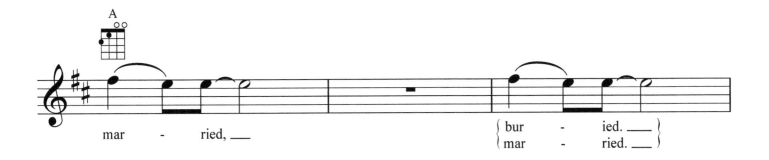

mar - ried, ___
{ bur - ied. ___ }
{ mar - ried. ___ }

Mar - ried, ___

bur - ied. ___ Yeah, yeah, yeah, yeah. ___

(Instrumental)

All a - lone ___ is all ___ we all ___ are. All a - lone ___ is all ___

___ we all ___ are. All a - lone ___ is all ___ we are. ___

All a - lone ___ is all ___ we are. ___

Additional Lyrics

2. I wish I was like you, easily amused.
   Find my nest of salt. Everything is my fault.
   I'll take all the blame, aqua seafoam shame.
   Sunburn with freezer burn. Choking on the ashes of her enemy.

Come as You Are

Words and Music by Kurt Cobain

Copyright © 1991 The End Of Music and Primary Wave Tunes
All Rights Administered by BMG Rights Management (US) LLC
All Rights Reserved   Used by Permission

Interlude
Em D Em D
1.–3.
Em D Em D
4.
D
D.S. al Coda
(take 2nd ending)
Coda
C Am
No, I don't have a gun.
C Am C
Outro
Em
No, I don't have a gun.
D Em D Em
Mem - o - ry, a
D Em D Esus4
4fr
mem - o - ry, a...

Drain You

Words and Music by Kurt Cobain

Copyright © 1991 Primary Wave Tunes and The End Of Music
All Rights Administered by BMG Rights Management (US) LLC
All Rights Reserved   Used by Permission

Dumb

Words and Music by Kurt Cobain

Copyright © 1993 The End Of Music, Primary Wave Tunes and BMG Platinum Songs
All Rights Administered by BMG Rights Management (US) LLC
All Rights Reserved   Used by Permission

Heart Shaped Box

Words and Music by Kurt Cobain

Copyright © 1993 BMG Silver Songs, The End of Music, BMG Platinum Songs and Primary Wave Tunes
All Rights Administered by BMG Rights Management (US) LLC
All Rights Reserved   Used by Permission

I wish I could eat ___
Throw ___ down your um - bil -

___ your can - cer when ___ you ___ turn black. ___
- i - cal noose ___ so I can ___ climb ___ right back. ___

Chorus

Hey! ___ Wait! ___

I got a new com - plaint. For - ev - er in debt ___

___ to your price - less ad - vice. ___ Hey! ___ Wait! ___

I got a new com - plaint. For - ev - er in debt ___

to your price - less ad - vice. ___ Hey! ___ Wait! ___

I got a new com - plaint. For - ev - er in debt ___

to your price - less ad - vice, ___ your ad - vice. ___

___ your ad - vice, ___

Outro

your ad - vice, ___

your ad - vice. ___ *(Instrumental)*

In Bloom

Words and Music by Kurt Cobain

First note

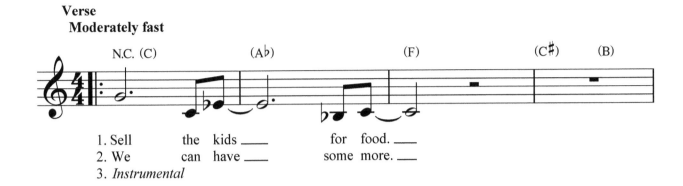

Copyright © 1991 Primary Wave Tunes and The End Of Music
All Rights Administered by BMG Rights Management (US) LLC
All Rights Reserved   Used by Permission

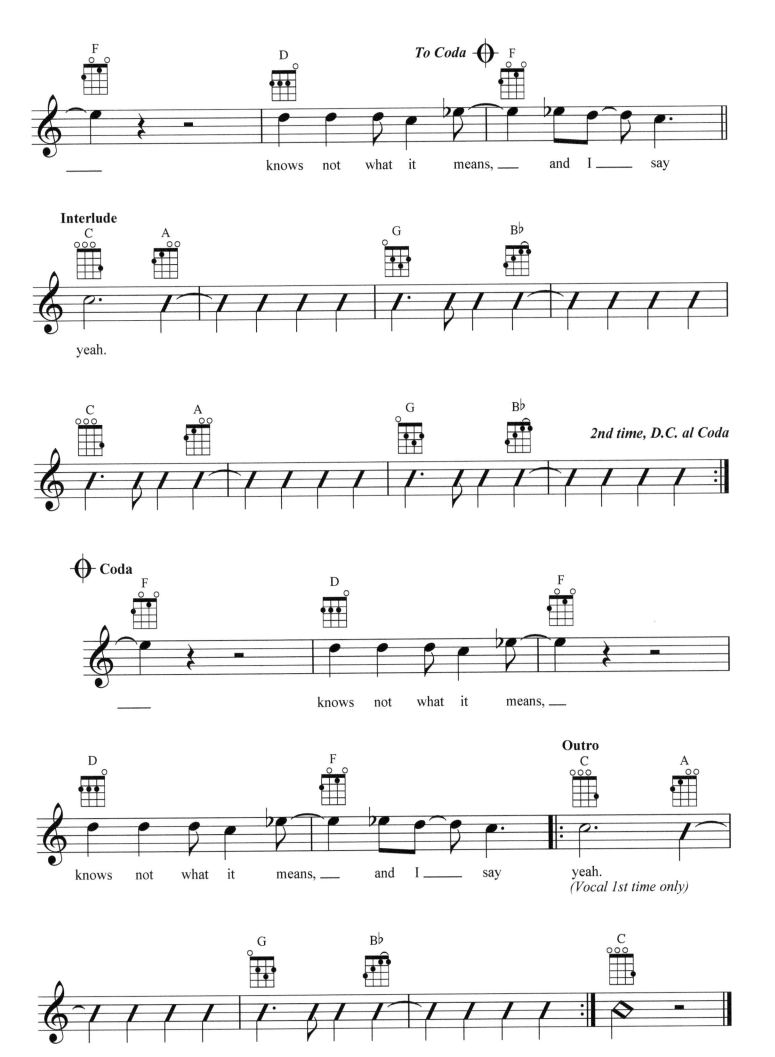

knows not what it means, ___ and I ___ say

Interlude

yeah.

2nd time, D.C. al Coda

Coda

knows not what it means, ___

Outro

knows not what it means, ___ and I ___ say   yeah.
(Vocal 1st time only)

Lake of Fire

Words and Music by Curt Kirkwood

Chorus
Moderately slow

Where do bad folks go when they die? They don't go to heav-en where the an-gels fly. _____ Go to a lake _____ of fire and fry, see 'em a-gain _____ till the Fourth of Ju - ly.

Interlude

© 1994 MEAT PUPPETS MUSIC (BMI)/Administered by BUG MUSIC, INC., A BMG CHRYSALIS COMPANY
All Rights Reserved   Used by Permission

Additional Lyrics

2. People cry, people moan,
Look for a dry place to call their home.
Try to find someplace to rest their bones,
While the angels and the devils try to make 'em their own.

Lithium

Words and Music by Kurt Cobain

First note

Verse
Moderately

1., 3. I'm so hap - py 'cause to - day ___ I found ___ my friends;
2. I'm so lone - ly; that's o - kay, ___ I shaved ___ my head ___

___ they're in my head. ___ I'm so ug - ly; that's o - kay, ___
___ and I'm not sad. ___ And just may - be I'm to blame ___

___ 'cause so ___ are you. ___ Broke our mirrors. ___ Sun - day
___ for all ___ I've heard; ___ I'm not sure. ___ I'm so ex -

morn - in' is ev - 'ry day ___ for all ___ I care; ___ I'm not scared. ___
cit - ed; I can't wait ___ to meet ___ you there, ___ but I don't care. ___

___ Light my can - dles in a daze, ___ 'cause I ___ found God.
___ I'm so horn - y; that's o - kay, ___ my will ___ is good.

Copyright © 1991 The End Of Music and Primary Wave Tunes
All Rights Administered by BMG Rights Management (US) LLC
All Rights Reserved   Used by Permission

I'm not gon - na crack. I'd kill you, — I'm not gon - na crack.

I like it, — I'm not gon - na crack. I miss you, —

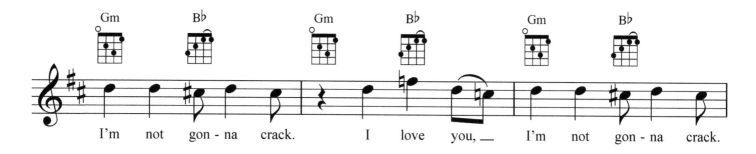

I'm not gon - na crack. I love you, — I'm not gon - na crack.

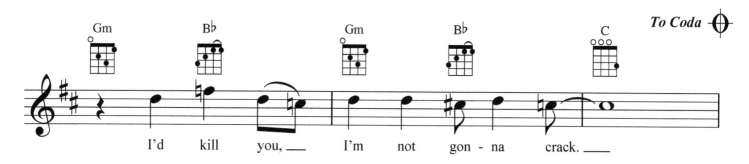

I'd kill you, — I'm not gon - na crack. —

Interlude

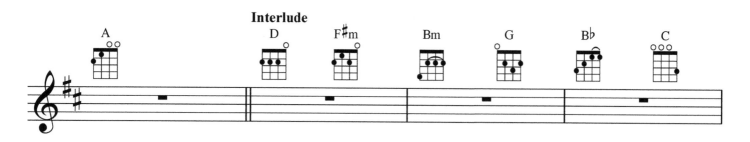

D.C. al Coda
(no repeat)

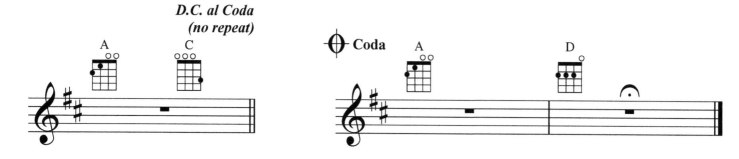

On a Plain

Words and Music by Kurt Cobain

Copyright © 1991 Primary Wave Tunes and The End Of Music
All Rights Administered by BMG Rights Management (US) LLC
All Rights Reserved   Used by Permission

The Man Who Sold the World

Words and Music by David Bowie

© 1971 (Renewed 1999) EMI MUSIC PUBLISHING LTD., TINTORETTO MUSIC and CHRYSALIS MUSIC
All Rights for EMI MUSIC PUBLISHING LTD. Controlled and Administered by SCREEN GEMS-EMI MUSIC INC.
All Rights for TINTORETTO MUSIC Administered by RZO MUSIC
All Rights for CHRYSALIS MUSIC Administered by CHRYSALIS MUSIC GROUP INC., A BMG CHRYSALIS COMPANY
All Rights Reserved   International Copyright Secured   Used by Permission

came as a sur - prise. ____ I spoke in - to his
gazed a gaze - ly stare. ____ We walked a mil - lion

eyes, "I thought you died a - lone a long, long time a - go." _
hills. I must have died a - lone a long, long time a - go." _

Chorus

____ Oh no, _____ not me. ____ We
____ Who knows? __ Not me. ____ I

nev - er lost con - trol. ____ You're face ____ to face ____ with the

Interlude

man who sold ___ the world. *(Instrumental)*

To Coda ⊕

1.

2.   ***D.S. al Coda***
(Lyric 2)

⊕ **Coda**

Who knows? _

rit.

Pennyroyal Tea

Words and Music by Kurt Cobain

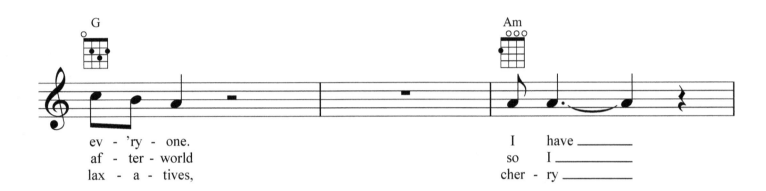

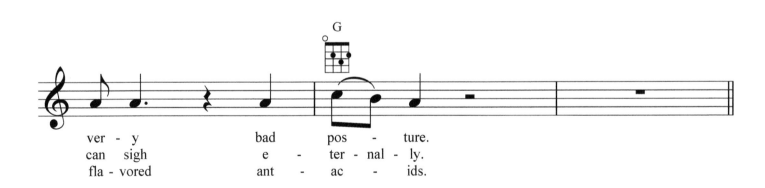

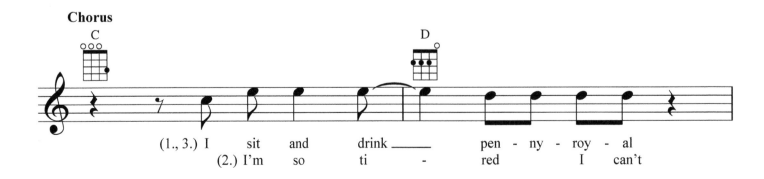

Copyright © 1993 The End Of Music and Primary Wave Tunes
All Rights Administered by BMG Rights Management (US) LLC
All Rights Reserved   Used by Permission

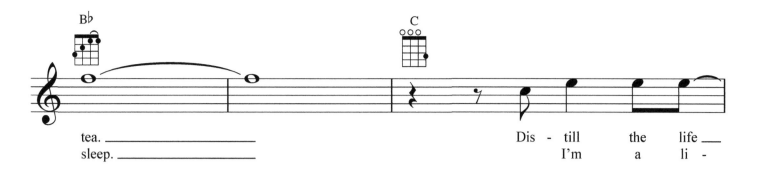

tea. _____

sleep. _____ Dis - till the life ___

I'm a li -

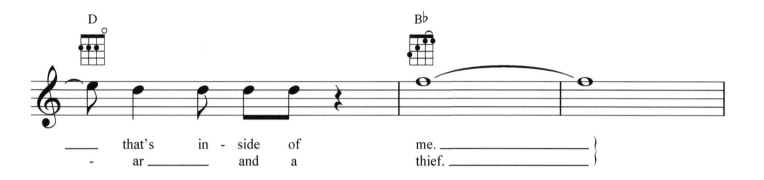

_____ that's in - side of me. _____

- ar _____ and a thief. _____

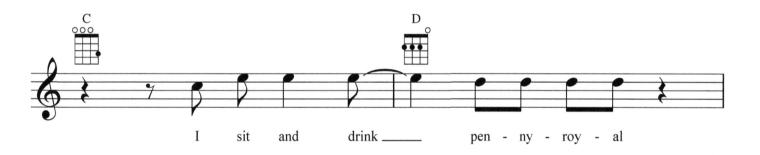

I sit and drink _____ pen - ny - roy - al

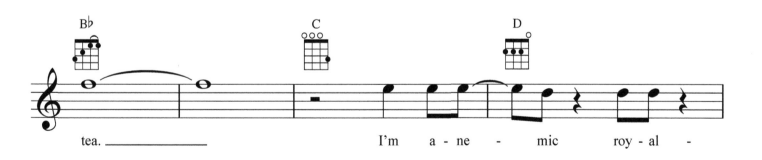

tea. _____

I'm a - ne - mic roy - al -

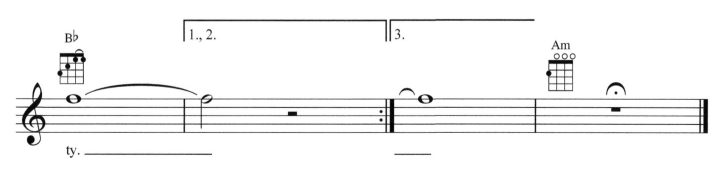

1., 2. | 3.

ty. _____

(New Wave)
Polly

Words and Music by Kurt Cobain

Copyright © 1991 Primary Wave Tunes and The End Of Music
All Rights Administered by BMG Rights Management (US) LLC
All Rights Reserved   Used by Permission

Rape Me

Words and Music by Kurt Cobain

First note

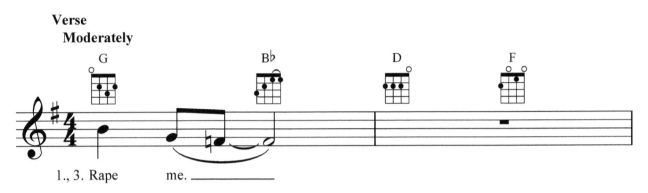

Verse
Moderately

1., 3. Rape me. _____

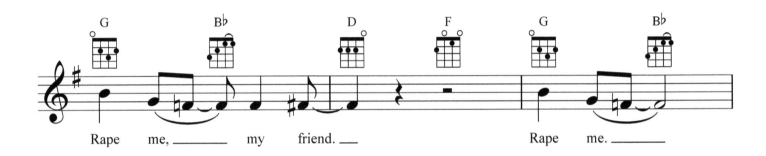

Rape me, _____ my friend. _____ Rape me. _____

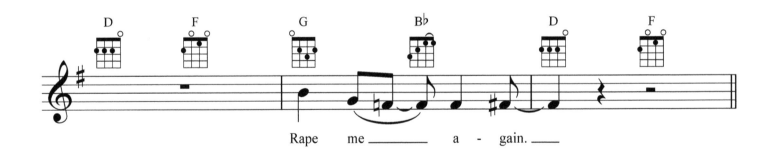

Rape me _____ a - gain. _____

Chorus

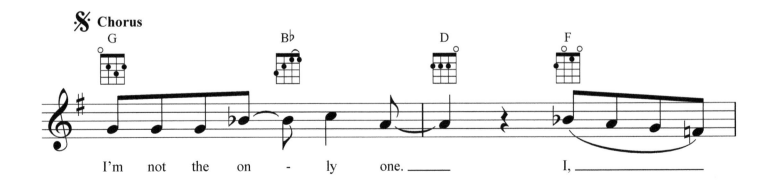

I'm not the on - ly one. _____ I, _____

Copyright © 1993 BMG Silver Songs, The End Of Music, BMG Platinum Songs and Primary Wave Tunes
All Rights Administered by BMG Rights Management (US) LLC
All Rights Reserved   Used by Permission

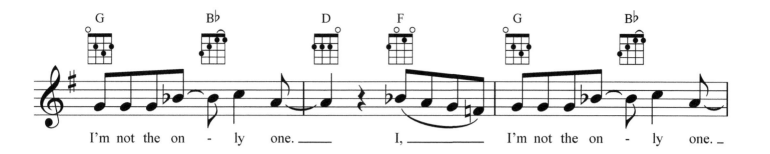

I'm not the on - ly one. _____ I, _____ I'm not the on - ly one. _

To Coda 1

To Coda 2

_____ I, _____ I'm not the on - ly one. _____

Verse

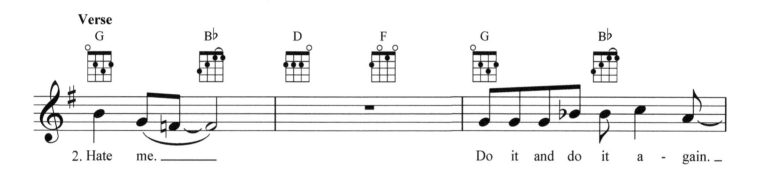

2. Hate me. _____ Do it and do it a - gain. _

_____ Waste me. _____

D.S. al Coda 1

Rape me, _____ my friend. _____

37

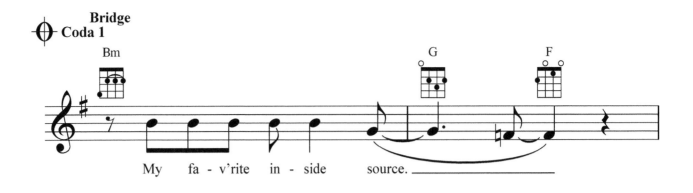

My fa - v'rite in - side source. _____

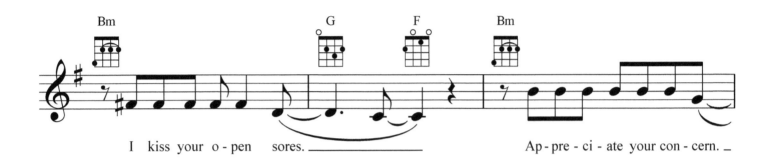

I kiss your o - pen sores. _____ Ap - pre - ci - ate your con - cern.

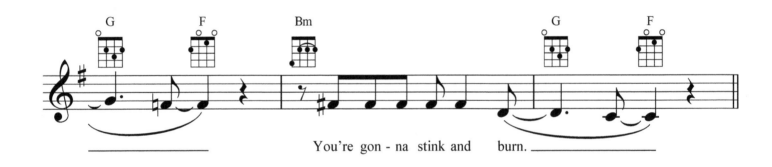

_____ You're gon - na stink and burn. _____

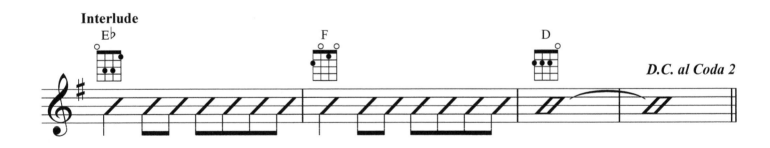

D.C. al Coda 2

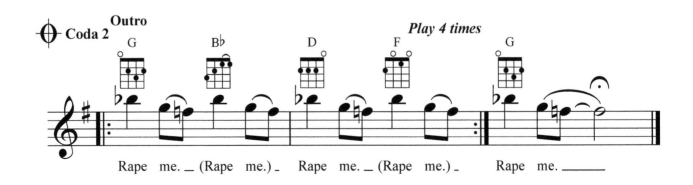

Rape me. _ (Rape me.) _ Rape me. _ (Rape me.) _ Rape me. _____

Smells Like Teen Spirit

Words and Music by Kurt Cobain, Krist Novoselic and Dave Grohl

Copyright © 1991 The End Of Music, Primary Wave Tunes, M.J. Twelve Music and Murky Slough Music
All Rights for The End Of Music and Primary Wave Tunes Administered by BMG Rights Management (US) LLC
All Rights for M.J. Twelve Music Administered by Warner-Tamerlane Publishing Corp.
All Rights Reserved   Used by Permission

Chorus

Additional Lyrics

2. I'm worst at what I do best,
   And for this gift, I feel blessed.
   Our little group has always been
   And always will be until the end.

3. And I forget just why I taste.
   Oh yeah, I guess it makes me smile.
   I found it hard; it's hard to find.
   Oh well, whatever... never mind.

Sappy

Words and Music by Kurt Cobain

1. And if you save your-self, you will
2., 3. *See additional lyrics*

make him hap-py. He'll keep you in a jar,

then you'll think you're hap-py. He'll give you

breath - ing holes, then you'll think you're hap-py.

He'll cov - er you with grass, then you'll

Copyright © 1989 Primary Wave Tunes and The End Of Music
All Rights Administered by BMG Rights Management (US) LLC
All Rights Reserved   Used by Permission

Chorus

think you're hap - py now. You're in a

laun - dry room. You're in a laun - dry room.

Con - clu - sion came to you, oh.

Additional Lyrics

2. And if you cut yourself,
   You will think you're happy.
   He'll keep you in a jar,
   Then you'll make him happy.
   He'll give you breathing holes,
   Then you'll think you're happy.
   He'll cover you with grass,
   Then you'll think you're happy now.

3. And if you fool yourself,
   You will make him happy.
   He'll keep you in a jar,
   Then you'll think you're happy.
   He'll give you breathing holes,
   Then you will seem happy.
   You'll wallow in the sh*t,
   Then you'll think you're happy now.

Sliver

Words and Music by Kurt Cobain

Copyright © 1989 Primary Wave Tunes and The End Of Music
All Rights Administered by BMG Rights Management (US) LLC
All Rights Reserved   Used by Permission

stop your cry - in'. Go out - side and ride your bike. That's what I did; I

Chorus *Play 3 times*

killed my toe. Grand - ma, take me home. Grand - ma, take me home.

Verse

Grand - ma, take me home. Grand - ma, take me home. 4. Af - ter din - ner I

had ice cream. I fell a - sleep and watched T - V. I woke up in my

Outro-Chorus *Play 9 times*

moth - er's arms. Grand - ma, take me home. Grand - ma, take me home.

Grand - ma, take me home, wan - na be a - lone.

Something in the Way

Words and Music by Kurt Cobain

First note

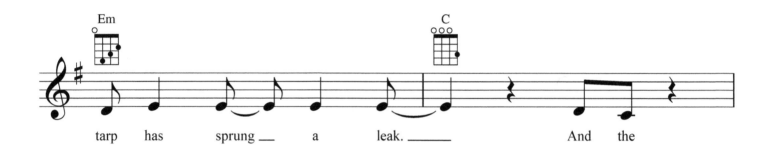

Un - der - neath ___ the bridge, ___ the

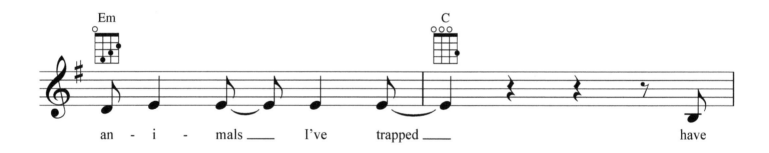

tarp has sprung ___ a leak. ___ And the

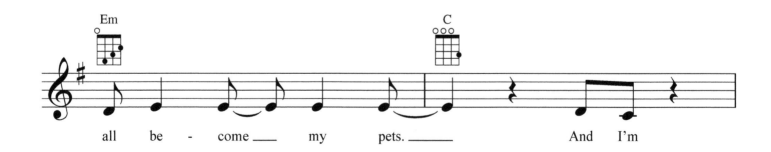

an - i - mals ___ I've trapped ___ have

all be - come ___ my pets. ___ And I'm

Copyright © 1991 Primary Wave Tunes and The End Of Music
All Rights Administered by BMG Rights Management (US) LLC
All Rights Reserved   Used by Permission

liv - ing off ___ of grass ___ and the drip - pings from ___ the ceil -

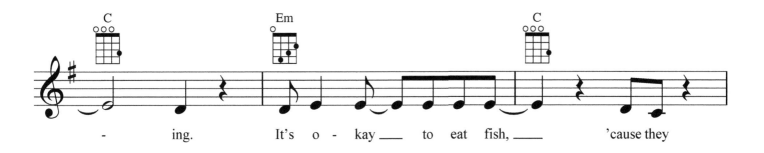

- ing. It's o - kay ___ to eat fish, ___ 'cause they

Chorus

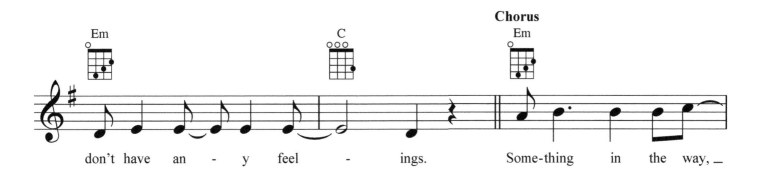

don't have an - y feel - ings. Some - thing in the way, __

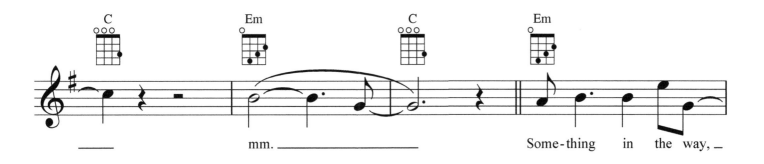

_____ mm. _____ Some - thing in the way, __

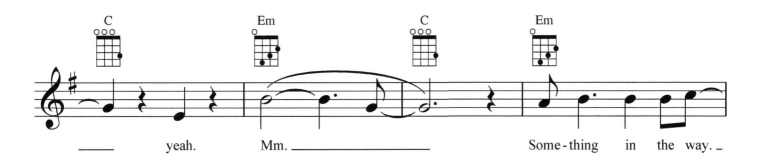

_____ yeah. Mm. _____ Some - thing in the way. __

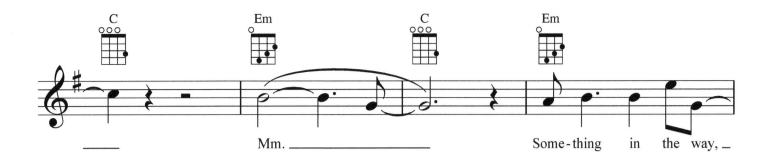

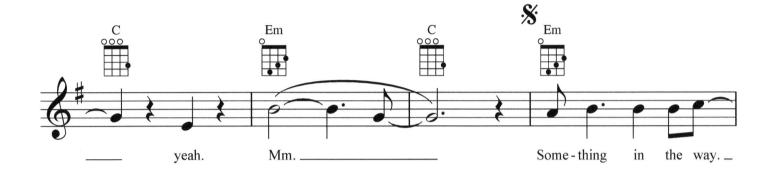

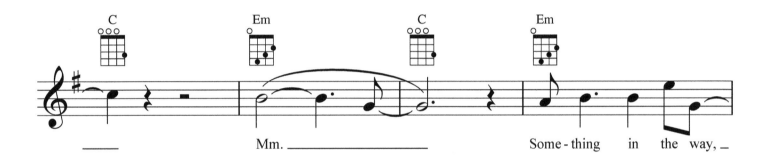

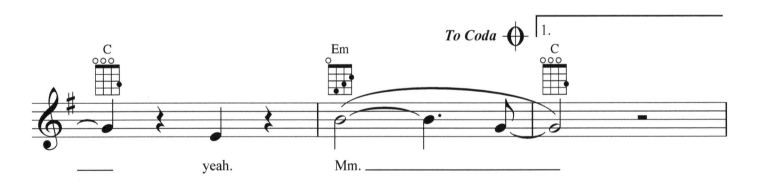

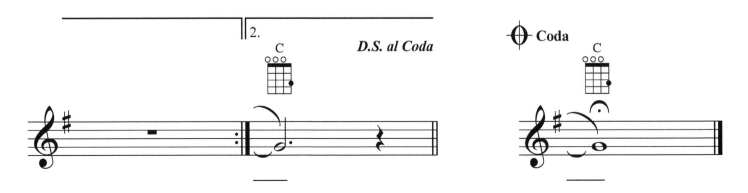

Where Did You Sleep Last Night

New Words and New Music Adaptation by Huddie Ledbetter

TRO - © Copyright 1963 (Renewed), 1995 Folkways Music Publishers, Inc., New York, NY
International Copyright Secured
All Rights Reserved Including Public Performance For Profit
Used by Permission

To Coda ⊕ | 1.–4. |

A   D

shiv - er _____ the whole night through.   2. My
shiv - er _____ the whole night through.   3. Her
bod - y _____ nev - er was found.   4. My
    5. *Instrumental*

| 5.

D   **D.S. al Coda**   ⊕ **Coda**   D

Instrumental ends   6. My   through.   7. My

Verse

D   Asus4   G   F

girl, my girl, don't lie _____ to me. Tell me:
(8.) girl, my girl, where will _____ you go? I'm __

A   D

where did you sleep last night? }
go - in' where the cold wind blows. }
    In the

Asus4   G   F

pines, in the pines, where the sun __ don't ev - er shine, I would

50

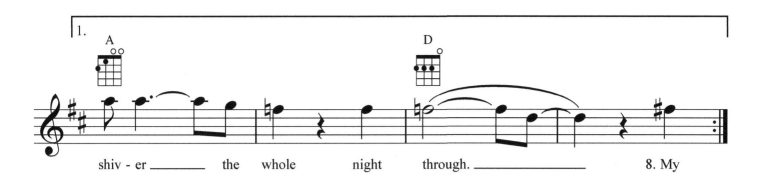

shiv - er _____ the whole night through. _____ 8. My

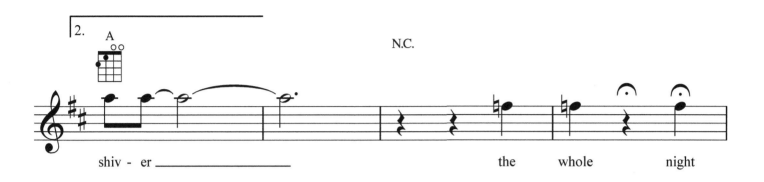

shiv - er _____ the whole night

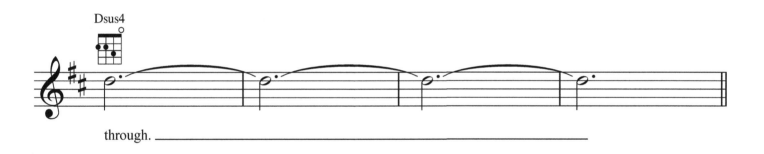

through. _____

Outro

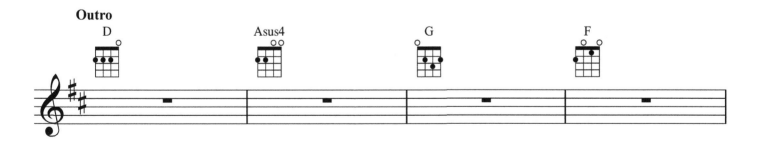

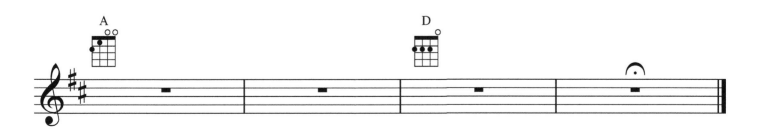

You Know You're Right

Words and Music by Kurt Cobain

First note

Verse
Moderately

1. I will nev-er both - er you.   I will nev-er prom - ise to. __

I will nev-er fol - low you.   I will nev-er both - er you.

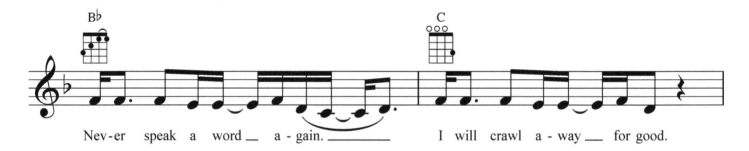

Nev-er speak a word __ a - gain. _____   I will crawl a - way __ for good.

I will move a - way __ from here.   You won't be a - fraid __ of fear.

No thought was put in - to this,   I al-ways knew it would come __ to this.

Copyright © 2002 Primary Wave Tunes and The End Of Music
All Rights Administered by BMG Rights Management (US) LLC
All Rights Reserved   Used by Permission

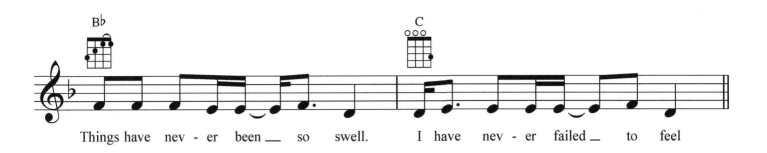

Things have nev - er been __ so swell. I have nev - er failed __ to feel

Chorus

pain, _____ pain, _____

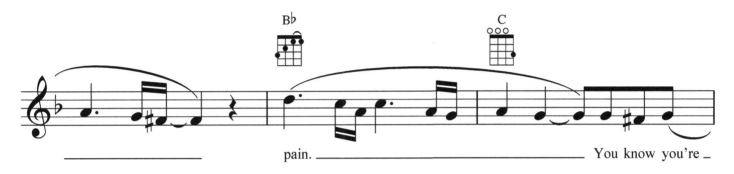

_____ pain. _____ You know you're __

__ right. _____ You know you're __ right. __ You know you're __ right. __

Verse

2. I'm so warm and calm __ in - side. I no long - er have __ to hide. __

Let's talk a - bout some - one else. __ Steam - ing Sue be - gins __ to melt. __

Noth-ing real-ly both - ers her, she just wants to love __ her-self. __

I will move a-way __ from here. You won't be a-fraid __ of fear. __

No thought was put in - to this, I al-ways knew it'd come __ to this. __

Things have nev-er been __ so swell. __ I have nev-er failed __ to feel

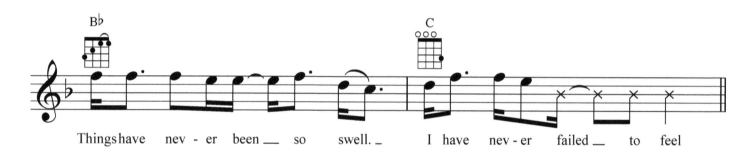

Chorus

pain, _____

pain, _____

54

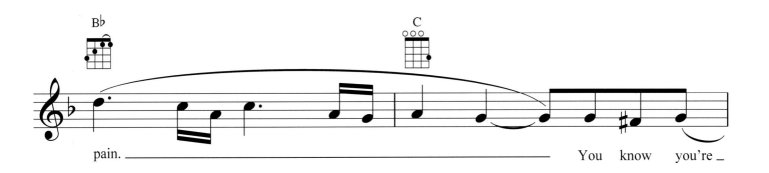

pain. _____ You know you're __

__ right. __ You know you're __ right. __ You know you're __ right. You know you're __

__ right. _____ You know you're __ right. _____ You know you're __

Outro

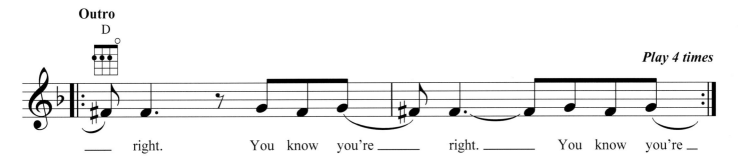

Play 4 times

__ right. __ You know you're _____ right. _____ You know you're __

__ right. __ You know your __ rights. __ You know your __ rights. You know your __

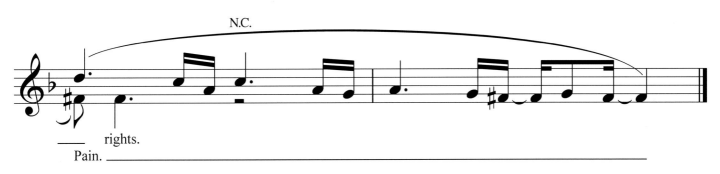

__ rights.
Pain. _____